Patterson Leonard McKinnie

Give a Lift to Mortals

And Other Poems

Patterson Leonard McKinnie

Give a Lift to Mortals
And Other Poems

ISBN/EAN: 9783744705127

Printed in Europe, USA, Canada, Australia, Japan

Cover: Foto ©Thomas Meinert / pixelio.de

More available books at **www.hansebooks.com**

Yours Sincerely
P. L. M. Kinnie

GIVE A LIFT TO MORTALS

AND OTHER POEMS

BY
DR. P. L. McKINNIE

ILLUSTRATIONS
BY
FLORENCE JOHNSON AND SARA CROSBY.

CHICAGO

CONTENTS.

NOTE.

The poems in this book except "For the Blue and the Gray" and "Blue Eyes and Violets" are selected from a volume of poems previously published by the same author, entitled "From Tide to Timber-Line.

TO MY WIFE.

When you give a lift to mortals who are walkin' in the shadder
Of a sorrow, an' you lighten it an' make their hearts beat gladder
You will be one round up higher, up higher on God's ladder,
    Toward his heaven every day.

Ibid, page 31.

GIVE A LIFT TO MORTALS

AND

OTHER POEMS.

WHO DUTY PARRIES NOT.

WHO is pure in heart, and duty parries not,
  Nor ever seeks an easy path
  By compromise with evil, hath
A destiny of conflict and a warrior's lot.
  Victory shall come to him
  Only on the death within

His heart of selfishness and lust, and greed
  Of gain. Evil tempts with gold,
  Or preferment, or threatens bold.
So should his courage have the greater meed
  Of truth: that armored mail
  The shafts of Evil shall assail

In vain, and broken lie at feet of Victory won,
   With Right, and purity of heart
   And purpose, shall courage ne'er depart;
But, putting on the buckler day by day, all duty done,
   The Victor's crown is won at last,
   Worthily, when the contest's past,

To be worn as jewels that shall be a crown
   Of truth and courage pure,
   With noble aspirations to endure
Unto the end.   Then may he lay all burdens down,
   And in sweet silence. peaceful rest
   With Him who doeth all things best.

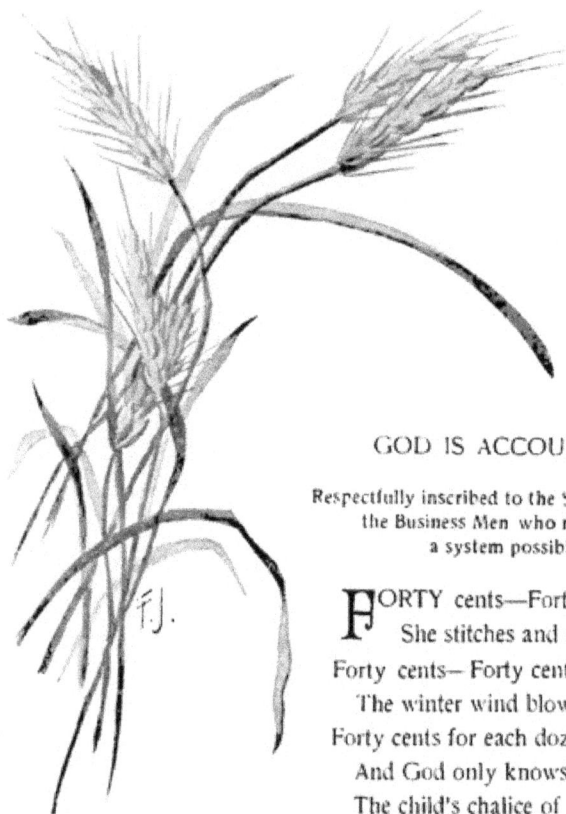

GOD IS ACCOUNTING.

Respectfully inscribed to the Sweaters, and to
the Business Men who make such
a system possible

FORTY cents—Forty cents—
  She stitches and sews.
Forty cents— Forty cents—
  The winter wind blows !
Forty cents for each dozen,
  And God only knows
    The child's chalice of woes.

Hands weary and red,
Cheeks pale as the dead;
  She is fourteen years old—
Forty cents—She's a working girl,—
Let her brain weary whirl,—
Slave to a miser churl
  Hoarding up gold.

She stitches and sews.
Life ebbs, never flows.

Want plowing furrows,
Disease making burrows,
   She is fourteen years old.
Heed not her imploring look,
Fear not the warning book ;
God's poor—and his wrath to brook—
   Grind to get gold.

She stitches and sews,
Life ebbs, never flows.
   Only fourteen years old,—
While on her face you read
Hope's death, and bitter need.
Misery for her decreed
   Adds to your gold.

   She is fourteen years old.
Grind her down till sore want,
Insatiate and gaunt,
Drives her to the haunt
   Of vices untold.
Then, Christians, pray for her,
While fiends lay snare for her,
None then to care for her,
   All hoarding gold.

   Forty cents—Does she sweat ?
   Canst thou, Christ, forget ?
Forty cents—Where are the preachers ?
She is one of Christ's creatures,
She is wearing his features—

.

"Fourteen years old."
They forget when he turned
The money tables and spurned
The sweaters who yearned
    To hoard up more gold.

Forty cents for the working girl;
Let her brain fevered whirl,—
    Lips growing white almost as the snows.
    She is only fourteen, and dying, but sews;—
Sews where disease and vice ever dwell;
Sews in a den that's the threshold of hell,
    That you may gain gold.
    Though your soul may be sold.

    Forty cents—she is counting—
    Forty cents—God's accounting.
Ah, here, here for her is fortune at last.
Her little heart throbbing, yet faster, more fast,
    Forty cents—she is counting—
"Five pennies for fare and five for bread,
    And five for—" "Forty cents, forty cents."
Then the notice was read.
The sewing girl's dead,
    And God is accounting.

PATRIOTS OF THE EMERALD ISLE.

OH, when, lovely isle of speech and of song,
    Oh, when shall be surcease of thy bitter wrong?
Thou hast drained to the dregs War's chalice of woes,
Of Famine, of Slaughter, and sore feudal blows;
And misrule and greed are joined hand in hand
To decry and despoil thy once happy land,
To poverty-shakle thy warm-hearty race,
And evil and law join hands in the chase.

For Hungary bleeding, for Greece when she cried,
Thy people shed blood, thy sons for them died.
Where Freedom has struggled through hundreds of years,
No land and no tongue plead in vein to thy ears.
From the fields of the Boyne, through the zones of the world,
To her throne, Appomattox, has Freedom unfurled
Her banner; but there he has rallied and died
For the boon that his own native isle is denied.

Oh, bring then, the shamrock, and cover his grave,
From the green hills of Erin, the land he would save;
While his soul with brave Emmet's inspiration will bring
So long as the bells of loved Shannon shall ring.
His voice for his native land cannot be hushed.
The truth to the earth can never be crushed;
From the grave he shall speak, with unpalsied tongue,
And the wrongs of the Emerald Isle shall be sung
In the name of her martyrs, till at last, on her crest,
In a halo of peace, shall her liberty rest.

TWO ENCAMPMENTS.

ALL hail! comrades, noble G. A. R.,
 From clime to clime, from near and far,
From pole to pole, and Orient come,
With banner and fife, and stirring drum,
With patriot heart-beat, all fall in.
Let the quick pulse throb at reveille's din,
And the broad Sierra's echo clear
The Grand Encampment's roll-call "here."

To comradship a tribute yield,
So dearly bought on battlefield,
In a pilgrimage to the golden gate,
Where story of field and camp await.—
In the regal splendor of Pullman cars,—
For they "tramp" no more, the G. A. R.'s—
High over the summit's rocky divide,
Where the eagle soars, to safely glide;

From the Royal Gorge to timber-line,
Through Castle Gate without countersign;
On the Marshall Pass the neighboring stars
Will greet in Review the G. A. R.'s;
And the sentinel peaks that "taps" ne'er know,
Will raise their hoary caps of snow
In grand salute to the men in blue,
Who, firm as they, stood staunch and true.

17

In the home of the clouds, where nature dies,
From the summits of earth to touch the skies,
And feel once more the phalanx unbroken.
Shoulder to shoulder, with no word spoken,
They may join our ranks who march no more,
For a moment of time from eternity's shore,
And the pledge that was sealed with the clasp of death
Shall be sworn again with the living breath,

While we hear in the winds the rustle of wings,
That a message from their encampment brings
To ours: that the battle is scarcely won,
And the pledges redeemed of '61,
For human rights, and justice true,
To the noble army of boys in blue;
For the sorrows of War have no surcease,
Save in justice only: "Let us have peace."

FOR THE BLUE AND THE GRAY.*

*In a shallow cut on the Nashville, Chattanooga and St. Louis Railway, between Altoona and Kenesaw Mountains, is the grave of an unknown soldier. The skeleton was discovered buried there some years after the war. It was impossible to determine whether he had been a Union or a Confederate soldier. The remains were reburied by the railway section hands close beside the track, and a tablet placed by the grave containing the words, "Unknown Soldier."

It will be remembered that it was from Altoona to Kenesaw Mountains that General Hooker flashed the signal to General Corse, "Hold the fort, for we are coming," on which was based the well-known hymn of that name.

The above lines were suggested to the author, who visited the grave on a recent trip to the south.

MEMORIAL.

SLEEPING the sleep that knows no awaking,
   Soldier unknown: what matters it now ?
Dumb is reveille when sunrise is breaking,
   Sleeping alone on Kenesaw's brow
From whence flashed the signal to Altoona's captain,
   " Hold to the fort, for I am coming now."

Sleeping the sleep of peace, weary soldier,
   In storm or in sunshine, in frost or the dew,
Unknown of name or unknown of army,
   Whether " blue " or the " gray," God knows he was true,
And He gave him welcome to bivouac celestial,
   In the fort that he holds for the " gray and the blue."

19

Undisturbed in his sleep on the highway of traffic,
   By the side of the rail that binds us anew,
The north and the south in bond of new union,
   Where all are united and loyal and true,
And as they pass by him, the north'ron or south'ron
   Drop a tear for the unknown, the " gray or the " blue."

No colors wave o'er him; no watchman on duty,
   Guarding the spot where he sleeps in the clay,
Save only the tribute of flowers in the springtime,
   From Kenesaw wafted by night and by day
On soft southern winds: the signal God's sending
   From the fort that He holds for the " blue and the gray."

ONE HUNDRED YEARS.

1776-1876.

GIVE retrospect a regal dower,
  Vouchsafed in conflict's crucial hour,
On field or forum where were cast
The lines that bind us to the past.

When souls of men bade men to stand
And offer lives for native land,
For Liberty, and hearthstone shrine,
Man's right, decreed by Will divine.

New stars are born of golden hue,
Intwined in folds red, white and blue;
A banner fills Aurora's skies,
The dawn of hope to waiting eyes:

Then comes a code that crowns a race,
And Saxon foes meet face to face,
At Lexington, on Bunker Hill.
Late Vassals, now are Kings at will.

Through jungles stained with loyal blood,
O'er Delaware's ice-gorging flood,
From hills of Maine to placid James,
The scroll is bright with valiant names.

" A yeoman race ! a yeoman King !
A Washington !" doth welkin ring.
With loud huzzas; through joys and tears,
The echoes fill a hundred years.

21

LOVE AND THE ROSE LEAVES.

A FRAGRANCE I, from Araby,
　　From vales of Cashmere captured,
From Occident, from Orient,
　An atmosphere enraptured.
　　　With odors sweet,
　　　I come to greet,
　Thy senses all caressing;
And, ravishing with pleasures meet,
　I bring to thee a blessing.

　　　　　My prison walls without portray,
　　　　　　By Art's deft hand reflected,—
　　　　　Rich roses rare, and blossoms fair,
　　　　　　In colors all perfected;
　　　　　　　And yet, behold,
　　　　　　　Lifeless and cold,
　　　　　Of rose flowers but a seeming
　　　　　　While I exhale, e'en from the mold,
　　　　　The essence of their dreaming.

And I, rose soul, live evermore
　With True Love, my handmaiden.
When sorely pressed, then I the more
　Give perfume richly laden.
　　　True Love and I
　　　Can never die:
Death proves but our perfection;
　And we do give nor plaint nor sigh
When crushed,—but fond affection.

I come, —the spirit of the flowers,—
　Intangible, yet token
Of hope, and faith, and vows that pass
　Through shades of death unbroken;
　　　All, thee I bring,
　　　On fragrant wing,
Love, love to thee confessing;
　May all thy life perennial spring
Be ever, is my blessing.

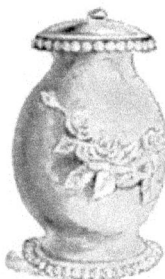

THE SHEEP ON THE COAST.

THE winds blow fierce from the hills to the sea:
　　But the rocks, like a fortress, shall keep
The wrath of the storm from the flock on the shore;
　　For the Master He loveth His sheep;

And they tranquilly rest in love and sweet peace,
　　And the lambs shall lie down and sleep;
For the storm by the Shepherd is tempered for them,
　　For the Master He loveth His sheep.

O weary, heartbroken, and storm-beaten soul,
　　There's a shelter for all who will seek,
And He heareth thy cry,—a hope unexpressed.
　　Oh! the Master He loveth His sheep.

The Rock that doth break the wrath of the sea,
　　And the Voice that doth quiet the deep,
Shall guard thee, and guide to a haven of rest.
　　Oh! the Master He loveth His sheep.

MY MOTHER.

THEY tell me she is dead.   That sainted face in life
        More saintly still in death,
        Changed only by a breath;
But she my mother still.   My soul, in strife
        With knowledge infinite
        And reason most finite,
Doth grope to know.   The dead to us are real;
        For, since I see her not,
        Her face is ne'er forgot;
And, in my soul, I know, and knowing, feel
        My mother's presence still:
        And so my finite will,
By reason throned, by faith is mastered well.
        Though she dead to nature be,
        Alas! she is not dead to me.
My beloved mother, who loved me, doth dwell
        Yet with me, sainted soul,
        Until the veil aside shall roll.
Her precepts, trusting God, henceforth shall ever be
        My guide; and, by them led,
        When others call me dead,
Then will she welcome me to God's eternity.

CELESTIA.

TO realms of love away, away,
      As radiant dawn to radiant day.
Than Ariadne fair, I ween,
Celestia rules a lovlier queen.

Eternal there a crown she wears;
Lo! in her hand a scepter bears.
A goddess pure, of love divine,—
All love bears tribute to her shrine;

And naught but joy beams from her eyes,
To lure e'en Love from Paradise.
In all the realms of Love ere this
None save Celestia's love is bliss.

THE BOON OF A BETTER LIFE.

*A*YE! bring sweet lillies, the pure white lillies
      And wreath the cross; for it is meet
To celebrate the new-born life
  With evergreens and blossoms sweet, –
      Fit emblem of the life to be
      Henceforth for you, from bonds now free,
      Who take the cross on bended knee.

"I baptise you in the name of the Father and Son;"
As thus He commanded, so hath it been done;
And I heard the voice of the pastor in prayer;
And I saw life's autumn and spring were there;
      And in evergreen words that will never decay,
      I read there is "joy in heaven to-day."
      While a still, small voice thus seemed to say:

"I will grant you the boon that you ask at my feet,
With the love of a child, so tender and sweet,
That will shine in your lives with joys that are blent
With the holiest love of the great firmament.

"I will give you a peace and purity bright
That will ever be with you, a beacon of light,
That others beholding, so faithful and true,
The path thou'rt pursuing they fain will pursue.

"I will give you a faith that from heaven is sent
To glow in the heart of the bowed penitent, –
A faith that is strong, and is broad and deep,
That in trials will keep you; yea, ever will keep.

"I will fill you with joys that are like honey-dew,
That, lasting forever, yet ever are new;
And the water of life, for a heritage ever,
I will give unto you that you thirst again never.

"I will give you a shield and a buckler and sword
That will keep you forever,—the sword of my word,
That will cheer you in age and guard you in youth;
'Tis the shield of devotion and buckler of truth.

"At last through the valley will I bring you to rest,
In the homes I have for you prepared with the blest;
And none shall be lost that to me have been given,
But all shall be with me in the kingdom of heaven."

GIVE A LIFT TO MORTALS

IF you do no shirkin' on the road you travel day by day,
   Of duty to your fellow-men you meet along the way
With burdens, but help bear them, you'll the great command
      obey,—
     That makes heaven every day.

You may know but very little 'bout creeds or any schism;
An', may be, can't repeat the long or shorter catechism;
But, when you wipe a tear away, you've found the greatest ism,
     And its heaven every day.
The big charity cotillon—if you ain't asked to lead it,
An' your name for charity ain't where the world will read it,
Just help down in the subsoil, where God's poor mostly need it,—
     You'll bring heaven every day.

Don't worry 'cause you can't build a school or seminary,
Or telescopes, or hospitals, or give a dispensary;
Just be content with doin' now the small and ordinary;
     For that is heaven every day.

Just a flower, a rose or lily, has saved a human bein',
An' a song or gentle music sent temptation backward fleein'
If you only do the mites of good, I know the Lord's agreein',
    It makes heaven every day.

If a child of want an' sorrow is wearyin' an' weepin',
An' in the dregs of sin an' shame all better nature steepin',
An' you lend a hand to help them, you're the best command-
        ment keepin'
    That is heaven right away.

So among the human stubble you can do His will a gleanin',—
Castin' not the gathered sheaves where, only, light is gleamin',—
An' help the fallen raise their eyes where love divine is beamin';
    And that is heaven every day.

When you give a lift to mortals who are walkin' in the shadder
Of a sorrow, and you lighten it an' make their hearts beat gladder,
You will be one round up higher, up higher on God's ladder,
    Toward His heaven every day.

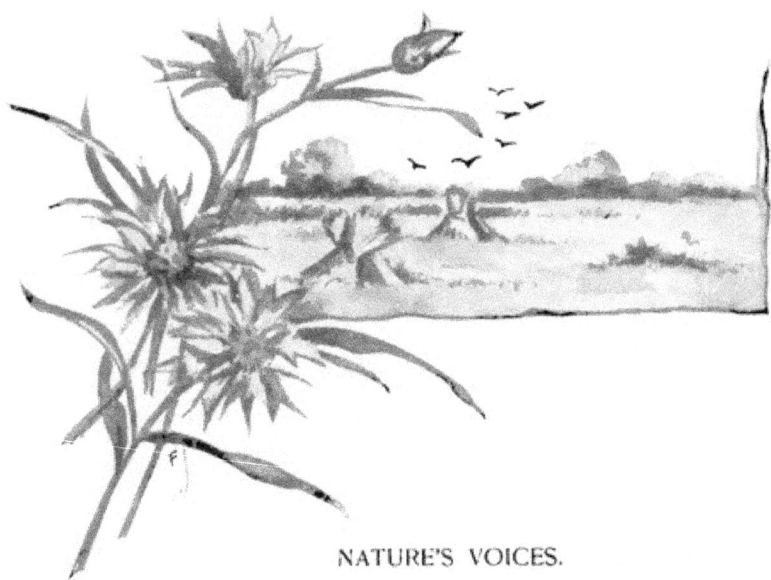

NATURE'S VOICES.

LESSONS all about me! voices of the truth!
    Ever are they speaking, fresh and bright as youth;

Written in the valleys, on the hills in verdure dress'd;
Carved in the deep Azoic,—upon the mountain crest;

Floating in the sunbeam, speaking in the flowers,
In silence on the desert, in Oriental bowers.

I read them in the woodland, in forests deep and old;
There, with the great Creator, I sweet communion hold.

By the voice of running water, in the rivulet and brook,
In the placid lake and torrent,—through all to Him I look.

He tells me in the mountain of His great power and might;
He gave me in the firmament a book to read by night.

In the blossom by the brooklet and frail nest just above,
He teaches me fidelity and sweet and tender love.

I see Him in the violet, I hear Him in the breeze;
In thunder tone He speaks to me in roar of mighty seas.

Some hear him in the cloister, I listen on the plain;
Some listen in the chancel, I hear Him on the main;

Some in the congregation of people, and but there,
Do hear him, but I hear him where echo speaks in air;

In the crystal and the cocoon, in the lignite and the leaf,
I read a revelation, and in reason my belief.

By the pulse that throbs within me, by the thought that's born of light,
By the power I feel that wins me, by the love that brings delight,—

By these lessons all I know Him, and by no less knoweth He
All creatures,—though below Him,—and thus He knoweth me.

And as the cloud or brooklet, to paths they once have trod,
Return no more forever, so end our lives with God.

SHERMAN AND PORTER MEMORIAL.*

* Read at a joint Memorial held in the Auditorium, Chicago, March 1st, 1891.

BRAVE soldiers born of Freedom's cause, tried sailors of the
deep,

Bear emblems of your sorrow, and warrior's honor keep!
Bring tributes of devotion, where, with reverential tread,
A nation comes uncovered, in the presence of her dead.
Float low the glorious banner, and the union jack o'er waves,
For them who sleep where Fame's videttes keep vigil
o'er their graves,—

For Sherman brave on native land, and Porter on the tide;
In peace and war, in life and death, twin patriots side by side.

The flag their valor glory gave, at half-mast shall it rest!
A signal from the mortal code, to immortals on the crest
Of ramparts in the Eternal, that other patriot souls
Have been summoned, and have answered to God's great muster-
rolls.

The farewell volley in the air, a knell within our breasts
Re-echoes from their honored graves, where all that's mortal
rests,
And wakes the memory of the day, that starts the silent tears,
And we battle and we bivouac in the record of the years

When clouds were lowering o'er the land and darkness on the
    deep;
And Lincoln's soul was agonized; and armies dared not sleep,
From Donelson and Shiloh to Atlanta's gauntlet run,
And Union flag and Union jack were defying Fisher's gun;

When the waters of the rivers were fettered by the hand
Of Mars, in strength of earth and steel, from James to Rio
    Grande,
With batteries masked and hidden, as by an Arctic night.
They came with souls in armored mail, of God's eternal right,--

Came as the whirlwind cometh from the open hand of God,
And broken shakles marked the path where mighty Freedom
    trod.
Then altars there were builded, and the sacrifice was laid,
For the Nation's great dishonor, that by fire and sword was paid.

On the shores of peaceful waters their prowess had released,
And giv'n to sea and Freedom with their heritage increased,
They have laid their bodies down; their souls have parried fears
And are marching to the minstrelsy of God's eternal spheres.

Then may all honored heroes' graves become the holy grail
Of a people reunited, and all loyalty prevail
In the name of hallowed peace, a tribute to the just,
Whose country's sword and honor were safest in their trust;

In peace or war true patriots, who spurned pretense, and gave
To all accord most justly, whether titled prince or slave,
Their whole lives teaching duty, as example only can,
That the loyal must be first of all a true American.

The galaxy of stars they sealed for union, law and land
In crimson of fidelity and white of virtue's band,
Shall nevermore be tarnished; but high o'er school and home
Shall ever float the signal flag of Freedom's sacred dome.

Ho! comrades and companions, and League of Tennessee,
Grand Sons of Revolution and Shipmates of the Sea,
Bring incense, all true patriots, all sons of loyal sires,
All maidens fair, all women true, and light the altar fires—

Of deep devotion to the flag, and fealty here renew,
By open graves of loyal men who to that flag were true
That with our honor and our lives, come weal or bitter woes,
We'll stand a wall of strong defense 'gainst seen or unseen foes.

In presence of the immortals, they are marching through the
    gate,
Where Lincoln, Grant and Farragut and Logan legions wait;
With heaven's sweet reveille their ranks are opening wide
To welcome Sherman, Porter there, true patriots side by side.

OUR COUNTRY AND FLAG.

EACH, with the other, unsullied, unbroken,
    Reflecting the deeds that have brought her renown,
Mankind's inspiration, of Freedom the token;
    Her yeomanry Kings. each wearing a crown.

FORGIVE, FORGET.

)ᴛHEN my weary days are past,
  And sleep doth end my labors,
And joy and fears are o'er at last,
  My record with my neighbors—
May it not be a granite shaft,
  Or epitaph's vain glory;
But, in their minds and hearts engraft,
This humble, simple story :

" He lived for those he loved always,
  He made his own their sorrows;
He filled love's chalice for to-days,
  And hope raised for to-morrows.
He craves no tears, no vain regret,
  No tribute, friends and brothers,
But only this, forgive, forget,
  His faults as he all others."

VIOLETS AND BLUE EYES.

ON the crest of Uncompaghre,
        Where the skies are bright and blue,
I plucked these wild wood violets,
    And send them, dear, to you.
        When I gazed upon their beauty—
            That was stolen from your eyes,—
                Then wantonly I plucked them,
                    And return to you the prize.

Then I sought—in vain—to capture
    The skies deep-stolen hue,
To return to its possessor
    Those eyes, your eyes, so blue.
But the glorious golden precept
    Of how "better 'tis to give
Than receive" then dawned upon me,
    And I prayed the flowers might live.

            For there's liquid blue and beauty,
                In the depths of those blue eyes,
            For all the flowers of springtime,
                For all the vernal skies,
            Which rob them not, but borrow,
                And the giving doth renew
            Those liquid orbs of beauty,
                Those eyes, your eyes, of blue.

38

ONLY A LIFE.

Only a ray in darkness,
    Only a fleeting breath,
Only a kiss and parting,
    Only from life to death.

Only a weary waiting,
    Only unknown to know,
Only desire and denial,
    Only to come and go.

Only a pain and patience,
    Only an ebbing tide,
Only a gleam of wisdom,
    Only a cause untried,

Only a call of waking,
    Only a sigh to sleep,
Only a tear, love's anguish
    Over a grave may weep.

Only a name forgotten,
    Only a hope at best,
Only a woe that's buried,
    Only a soul at rest.

THE ASSAYS THERE WILL ALL BE TRUE.

JIM Leonard stood–his pick and spade
  With poncho tied together—
Beside the grave where now is laid,
  From the world he could not weather,
His pard; and life was cold and drear
  In the camp of Twilight Canon,
For he was dead that for ten "year"
  Had been his boon companion.

The trail seemed lonely now to climb,
  The drills and anvils weighty;
He felt that age was marking time
  Upon his brow at eighty;
Now bleaker looked his prospect hole
  Than curtains dark of Kedar,
And, like the wail of a tortured soul,
  The winds sighed in the cedar.

At last he spoke as though in prayer,
  Or sadness broken hearted,
And these the words he uttered there,
  Addressed to the departed:
"Old pard, you're gone, and I'm alone:
  But, when the winds are sighin',
I seem to hear the parting tone
  I heard when you were dyin'.

"The waters down the canons pour,
  Like spirits vengeance wreakin',
And in the rattlin' thunder's roar,
  I think I hear you speakin';

Jim Leonard stood—his pick and spade
With poncho tied together.

And when at night I hear the slide,
 And trees and boulders fallin',
I'm thinkin', pard, you're by my side
 Or for me you are callin'.

"But now I'm gettin' tired of life,
 It grows more sad and weary;
The days are full of toil and strife,
 The silent nights are dreary;
And, pard, I soon will climb the trial
 That starts where peaks are endin'
And turnouts there we'll never hail,
 We meet no packs descendin'

"We'll climb the mountain sides no more,
 By night and day prospectin';
We'll file a claim for t'other shore,
 And wait the ressurectin';
An', if we never panned out here
 What we have been expectin',
We'll make our trail a title clear
 To callin' and electin'.

"My shift will soon be over, pard:
 I'll soon be done a stopin';
We'll all be under cover, pard,
 Where drifts are never slopin';
The levels all are on one base,
 No upper shifts a blastin';
The tunnels all meet in one place,
 The chamber's everlastin'

The trail seemed lonely now to climb.

"My Shift will soon be over, pard;
    I'll soon be done a stopin';
We'll all be under cover, pard,
    Where drifts are never slopin' "

"The assays there will all be true,
    Accordin' to our sample;
And when the mill runs are all through,
    They'll show us this example:
That if we work the jig below
    By 'saltin" and deceivin',
That up there, pard, there is no show
    To cover and get even.

"And when the sortin's all been done,
    And ready for the grindin',
I trust old pard, 'high number one,'
    They'll most of us be findin'
For concentration methods, pard,
    They've never up there boasted;
But down the chute low grade and hard
    Is crushed and dumped and roasted.

"But, pard, if we have rustled square,
    And never practiced jumpin'
The claims wherein we had no share,
    We needn't fear the dumpin';
For I believe that who has made
    The mountain has no failin's,
And he can find a better trade
    Than burning up the tailin's."

A BIRTHDAY GREETING

TO MY WIFE WITH A PRESENT OF JEWELS.

ONE thousand leagues afar from thee,
   My Love, from thee,—my love, from thee,—
On this thy natal day to be,
   My Love,—so far away to be!
And yet my love insatiate
Those leagues doth all annihilate,
   And I'm with thee,
   My love, with thee.

My heart sits prison breaks, My Love;
My love all distance scorns, my Love,—
   And far away it flies to thee,—
   It flies away with thee to be;
And on its wings this token bears,
And by its purity, Love, swears
   For thee,—for thee.
   Love,—swears for thee.

And wear it, Love, where it may feel
   Thy warm blood pulse with each heart-beat,
And back 'twill give with that appeal,
And, from its jewel depths, reveal
   The love I'd fain lay at thy feet.

And from those sparkling depths shall rise,
   Responsive to thy glances sweet,
Ecstatic bliss! love's sweet surprise,
That oft I've read in thine own eyes
   When thine and mine in rapture meet.

So may our love full rounded be,—
   All mine! all thine!—and without end,
Or ebb, or flow, but ever free
In one full realm of ecstacy
   And joy that love alone can blend.

And as these jewels brighter glow
   In darkest chambers, so I pray
Our love may sweeter, stronger grow,
Should fate a shadow o'er us throw,
   Till shadows end in endless day.

And so, my Love, though far from thee,
   So far from thee,
This day, I pray thou'lt happy be,
   Most happy be;
For greeting, Love, I send to thee,—
   Love's greeting unto thee,—
      To thee.

And may thy life with many days
  And years of joy full measured be,
With loving friends to cheer always,
  And sorrow's tears be far from thee.

And I would build within thy breast
  An altar pure, love's holy shrine;
Thy husband's love should be its crest,
  With fond devotion truly thine.

And so its fires should brightly burn,
  Enkindled by thy loving heart;
And from all else he'd ever turn
  To thee, nor from thee ever part.

Thy children's happy hours should be
  The daily incense offered there,
That, in their love's simplicity,
  Thou shouldst but read a daily prayer.

May loving kindness be thy star
  To guide thy life,—and mine and ours,
In all life's paths, so near, so far,
  Shall each and all have happy hours.

GOD CIPHERS ME AN' YOU.

THAR ain't no use o' talkin', boys,
    Thar's suthin' downright square
In how the laborin' fellers do
    When sorro' plows her share
Into the subsile ov the heart
    All racked with grief an' care.

An' boys, the way to jedge ov men
    Is by works, and not by creed;
For thar's suthin' square about 'em
    Who bind the hearts that bleed,
An' fer widows and fer orphans
    Provide in time ov need.

An' jist one month gone yistirday,
    It was that Reuben said
To me, as I was standin' thar
    Beside his dyin' bed,
That, ef his time had come, he knew
    His children would be fed.

An', while I held his hand in mine,
    I heerd him faintly say,
That blessin's would be theirn, he knew,
    Whose creed was more than pray;
An' then he said, "God bless the—"
    But he had passed away.

49

An', boys, the pledge they made to him,
  With her they all hev kept,—
An' more; fer through the fever's fire
  They rested not nor slept;
An' when't was vain, they with us all
  Thar tears ov sorro' wept.

      An', when her heart was breakin'
        With the comin' home to dwell
      Where the embers all was ashes
        On the hearth, an' where the knell
      Of emptiness was sadder
        Than the tollin' ov the bell

            When the shadder ov the valley
              Was black with clouds ov woe,
            They come with oil an' spik'nard,
              An', like colorin' ov the bow,
            They raised Hope's gleamin' banner,
              With its sweet an' radiant glow.

                So, then, I say, to jedge ov men,
                  If you would jedge 'em true,
                Is not so much by what they say
                  As by the deeds they do;
                An' I jist reckon, on this plan,
                  God ciphers me an' you.

THE TEMPERANCE MILLENNIUM.

THE millennium door is swingin',
   An' the better is gettin' the lead
Ov the bad, an' the men are beginnin'
   To show signs ov temperance feed;
An' men unto men are like brothers,
   Fer the Paradise Bird is their guest,
An' the children an' wives an' mothers
   Are prayin' they'll all be blest.

P'r'aps some ov 'em now will get dresses
   Who fer years but rags hev wore,
With huggin's an' lovin' caresses
   Where was growlin's an' kickin's before;
An' some little ones will find fathers,
   An' fathers lost children will find
Revealed in the tears that are fallin'
   Like scales droppin' off'n the blind.

I reck'n that now thar'll be prayin',
   Where thar hasn't been prayin' fer years;
Nor wantin' be found in the weighin'
   Nor pillows all soakin' with tears;
An' they'll eat the bread ov love's leav'n
   Who've been breakin' the crusts ov woe,
That'll be like a foretaste ov heaven
   Beginnin' on earth below;

An' manhood that long has been layin'
    Chained down in the ruinin' bowl,
Will put on the weapons fer slayin'
    The slayer ov body an' soul.
An' hearts that rejoice, I'm knowin',
    Are many an' pure an' true,
Baptized in the waters that's flowin'
    From the river ov life fer you.

An' the midnight watchin' an' weepin'
    In trouble an' want an' shame,
Will be changed fer dreamin' an' sleepin'
    By the hearth with a hallowed name;
In the home where sorrow's been sittin'
    Like a wolf fer many a day,
Will the Paradise Bird be flittin',
    An' buildin' her nest to stay.

Then the children will lisp a blessin',
    An' the wimmin will weep no more
For the days that were sad an' distressin'
    Are passin' fer joys in store,
While they pray fer the Guardi'n Angels
    To be with 'em, an' keep 'em alway
In the path where the wayside is plenty,
    An' the end is a golden day.

CRIPPLE TIM AND THE
CHARITY BALL.

'TWAS the eve of a brilliant charity
    ball;
The streets were gay, and the gorgeous hall
Was a blaze of glory,—and the spirit of all
Was for "charity's sake."
For often as ye to the least of these do,
    ye do unto Me.

By a cafe window "Cripple Tim" stood
Eagerly gazing through at the food,
Unnoticed by all on the busy street.
He looked on plenty, with nothing to eat
Then he turned and shouted, "Shines for all;
Shine 'em up free for the charity ball."

"Has the world lost pity?" a still voice speaks
And tears course down over Tim's pale cheeks
To lips that in days gone by had prayed
"Forgive us; and give us our daily bread,"—
Mocking words crushed out in the strife,
Remembered no more in his struggle for life.

Then, weary and sick, ragged and cold,
"Cripple Tim" climbed to his attic old,
  And found, in tears
   Only orphans weep,
  The balm for fears
   And hunger,—sleep.

In a fever's dream he beheld a star
From the east come guiding a glittering car
To his attic old,—with a beatiful maid
In dazzling spendors rich arrayed.
In her hands she carried a loaf and bowl;
Her lips and eyes brought food for the soul,
Yielding a harvest of multiplied love.
"Good will on earth" lays treasures above·
  Who gives shall receive,
   In a double fold,
  Heart treasures in sheaves
   That are richer than gold.

Then he murmured low: "Now, boys, let's all
Rub shines free gratis for the charity ball."
The mother of love spread out her wings,
And a song unheard the Dark Angel sings:
With its dying note the life cord broke;
He parted from men, but with God awoke.
  His box and brush
   Will know him no more:
  "Cripple Tim" spoke
   From the other shore.

The dark-winged angel had kissed his brow:
With the mother of love he resteth now;
He whispered the words, in passing to sleep,
"I know them who love me,—they feed my
        sheep."

Sweet music swelled from the banquet hall,
And life and love heard the Master's call.
The beautiful maid and the cavalier
In charity gave, the world to cheer.
There is gold enough for all.   The world
Most needs the banner of love unfurled
        In the heart of man,—
        The Christ-like plan.

LOVE'S FETTERS.

TO A FRIEND.

THERE may be others wish thee well,
   Or those who love thee fonder,
In summer fair, or wintry days;
   But none who stay or wander
Give tribute truer, worthy praise.
   Rejoice I in your pleasure,
Your happiness my prayer always,
   From measure unto measure.
Your wish the shrine of loving hearts
   Filled with thy smile— a blessing
Replete, and full in every part,
   Its silence but confessing
E'en all that love can give or take.
   Seek not a pledge or hostage;
Dissolve all bond or truce, and make
   Life one harmonious, rhythmic lay,
Embowered in sweetest roses
   Of true affection's lasting day;
Nor end when life's dream closes.

AMERICA, HOME LAND.

WE are standing in the glory of a galaxy of stars,
  On a field of blue emblazoned by the gleaming
Of camp fires that were lighted for freedom's holy wars,
  That the harvest of the years hath brought, redeeming.

And we shout a loud hosanna to America, home land,
  That shall echo to the end of all creation,
For our country reunited and redeemed to ever stand,
  For God and man, a freeman's happy Nation.

From the embers slowly dying in the ashes of the past,
  Behold a glow immortal is upspringing,
In the banner, crimson dyed with the blood of loyal men,
  Whose praises all the ages chord in singing.

Let the hills that flashed the code, and lagoons that answered
      back,
  In accord with hill and prairie sing the story;
Let the babe and mother sing, the sire and grandsire sing,
  And emancipated hosts proclaim the glory.

For the living brave who bear their country's wounds and
      scars,—
  All honor and all glory we award them;
For the loyal brave who sleep in the battle-grave of wars, —
  Immortelles, and flowers, and tears to-day accord them.

And all shout a loud hosanna to America, home land,
  That shall echo to the end of all creation,
For our country reunited and redeemed to ever stand,
  For God and man, a freeman's happy Nation.

PALMER LAKE COLORADO.

A GEM upon the crest she lies,
    Where pillared spires the ranges break,
Reflecting stars in noonday skies,
    The summit's jewel, Palmer Lake.

Killarney's and Geneva's shores
    No thrill so pure can e'er awake;
Here Freedom breaks all prison doors,
    And feasts the soul at Palmer Lake.

No legend sad thy beauty mars,
    Of clanking chains or feudal hate;
But from thy depths stars glance to stars
    Like kisses thrown from Palmer Lake.

Mount of the Holy Cross, and peak,
    Thy valiant guardians, stand, and break
The Storm King's wrath, that here shall wreak
    Not one coarse breath, sweet Palmer Lake.

Thy waters, clear as pure Siloam,
    For mirror would a goddess take;
And Cupid on thy shores his home,
    With Love, would choose, sweet Palmer Lake.

FIDELITY.

May it be so!
  And well,
In this deep woe
  To dwell.

My heart be wrung,
  And break
Of love that sprung
  To wake—

Upon the morn
  Of hate—
The wild, love-born,
  Fierce hate.

I can but pray
  " 'Tis well;"
I ne'er can say
  "Farwell."

My heart will cling
  To thee;
My love will spring
  To be—

Thine own e'ermore
  Then erst,
Thy passion o'er,
  To burst,—

As doth the rose,
  When prest,
Its sweet disclose;
  Then blest—

I'll deem my fate
  To live,
Love for thy hate
  To give.

EVANGELINE.

SHE comes on the wings of gladness,
  The fruition of hope's delight,
Like breaking of joy upon sadness,
  Like the dawn to an Arctic night;
Like dew to the thirsting desert,
  Like water to fountains dry,
Like love to love responding,
  With love that can never die.

THE GOD OF GOLD.

"It is easier for a camel to go through the
eye of a needle, than for a rich
man to enter into the
kingdom of God."

CUT them down, hoard your gold,
   Till your hearts' knell be tolled,
Till your souls have been sold
   To your god, godless gold.

Cut them down, gold to gain,
Though the tears fall like rain,
And you multiply pain
   By your scepter of gold,—

Men whom the morning's ray
Drives like beasts of prey
Down to their dens away,
   Deep in the earth,

To toil like the galley slave,
In vain their last rest to save
From scorn in pauper's grave,—
   Hoarding your gold.

Cut them down on the rail;
Let there be no avail
In the cry or the wail
   Of want in their homes;

61

Whom fear never knew,
By day and night true,
Though they brave death for you,
    Who worship but gold.

Cut them down at the bench,
At the forge, in the trench,
On the farm; turn the wrench,
    To gather more gold.

Cut them down yet again
Till you make tramps of men,
And thieves of tramps, when
    You worship but gold.

Heed not the imploring look,
Fear not the warning book;
God's poor, whom he ne'er forsook,
    Grind to get gold.

Spare none, young or old;
Till your hearts fill with mold,
For your souls have been sold
    To your god, godless gold.

LOVES DESPAIR.

HAVE you felt the quakings,
 The weary heart achings,
Of love that is spurned with bitterest scorn;
 And your faith but discloses,
 'Neath the smiles and the roses,
Deception there forging a life-piercing thorn?
 Have you drunk from loves chalice
 Woe, misery, and malice,
And Fidelity summoned no angel to warn?

 Has your soul, like a seabird
 When only woe's shriek is heard,
Been storm tossed from wave crest to wave crest
 Of woe, through a sea trough of gloom,
Back to the caverns of memory's wild unrest,
 Where stalks but the specter of doom,
And the heart beats the knell of hope in its breaking,
 Breaking and sinking to the lost spirits' lair,
Till you prayed for the sleep that knows no awaking,
 That only is solace for souls in despair?

THE SOLDIER.

GIVE honor to all to whom it is due,
 Who duty or death never parried;
But honor the soldier anew and anew
 Whose shoulder the bayonet carried.

www.ingramcontent.com/pod-product-compliance
Lightning Source LLC
Chambersburg PA
CBHW022027080426
42733CB00007B/763